Remembering Fireflies

Remembering Fireflies

Pamela Laskin

Plain View Press
P. O. 42255
Austin, TX 78704

plainviewpress.net
sb@plainviewpress.net
1-512-441-2452

Copyright Pamela Laskin, 2007. All rights reserved.
ISBN: 978-1-891386-98-5
Library of Congress Number: 2007942834

Cover art: Kirsi Tuomanen Hill
Photographs: Elizabeth Moskowitz
Photograph of Author: Michelle Valladares

Contents

Pregnancy   9

    The Abortion   11
    Different Rhythms   12
    In the Womb: Hearing a Baby's Heart-beat
       for the First Time   13
    Possibilities   14
    The Visitor   15
    Songs Of Mothers and Daughters   16
    Grass   17
    Family Of Infants   18
    Remembering Fireflies   19
    A Found Poem: The Ninth Month   20

Mothers and Grandmothers   21

    Rape   23
    Burns   24
    Without Mother   25
    Cancer   26
    A Fairy-Tale of Three Mothers   27
    After a Back Surgery   29
    A Mother's Daughter   30
    Sounds   31
    Kisses   32
    On Giving my Grandmother a Shower   33
    Songs   34
    At the Park   35
    Grandmother   36

Children   37

    To Woman With a Child   39
    On Babysitting For a Friend's Son   40
    The Diaphragm   41
    Foreplay   43
    Midas' Touch   44
    K.K.K.   45

A Parent's Nightmare	46
Untitled	47
Meningitis	48
A Woman and Her Lovers	49
Turn Off the Light	50
Bruises	51
Gifts	52
Disneyworld	54
About the World	55
Cross Country Skiing, Pound Ridge, February 1988	56
Distant Star	57
Fallen Tooth	58
Simply Just	59
Blind Batter	60
Overboard	61
Pollen	62
A Bike Ride with my Two Year Old	63
My Daughter's Music	64
The Naked Emperor	65
After Halloween	66
After Halloween II	67
Like Dreams	68
On the Evening of Halloween	69
Home	70
Be Thankful for. . .	71
About the Author	75
Acknowledgements	77

To my mother, Fran, and to all the mothers
and children in the world

And to Craig – this one is for you!

Pregnancy

The Abortion

It would be simple
to expel you;

in my grandmother's days
they used wire hangers,
while some girls
jumped up and down
certain
there'd be an accident.

I could walk
into a white-washed room
where a smiling doctor
wearing rubber gloves
could pinch and prod you

till you'd emerge
without finger or toenails;

but with hands as tiny as ladybugs,
and legs, curled,
like a hemorrhaged rose.

Different Rhythms

My student is pregnant
same time as me,
writes in her journals:
daily I swell
with the anguish of a storm-cloud;

I pass on my old clothes
and words to her:
"Good detail."

We grow
together
in verse
an unrhymed couplet.

But who could give shape
aside from myths, perhaps,
to this larger element
which replaces stomach and intestines;

she will one day burst
with a poem very different from my own:

blonde haired, blue eyed
free verse.

In the Womb: Hearing a Baby's Heart-beat for the First Time

Like a dream
not sure of
where it's going
but enjoying itself too much
to awaken you;

it throbs
beneath the surface
as if noises

are bubbling
out of a swamp.
Such delicate threads
out of this luscious mud

that you wish
this were forever
this moment

when this splendid child
first let you know
I am.

Possibilities

If I told you
there's someone in my belly
who, thirty years from today,
April 14, 1988
in a new century, in fact
this nameless, sexless person
could grow to be anything, anyone
and might be mensch enough
to stop Exxon from spilling oil
into our clear, blue oceans,
or perhaps could put an end
to an administration that says
unwanted babies should be born;

if I told you all of this
you wouldn't believe
such a miracle
could happen,
but remember:
in the 21st century
to which I thrust this beautiful baby
out into the world,
anything
and everything
is possible.

The Visitor

In your eighth month your body
is no longer your own. You
try to breathe and hear only
a bird's call, small and faint
in winter.

The morsels you eat
are not just for you. You swallow
a bite, and it quickly disappears.
Only the burning in your chest
tells you that you've eaten.

When you walk, two bodies,
your torso lower to the ground,
you fish for the old self:
some note in the pocket,
the remnants of a waist
you'll never find.

Perhaps in the ninth month
you'll ask the visitor
who has inhabited your studio
for so long
to move out;
even when he does, so I've heard
he never leaves.

Songs Of Mothers and Daughters

I tell my husband
you kick all night
like my stomach
is a punching bag;
he says in jest
to kick you back.

I spent years like that, with my mother.
I moved adeptly like a tightrope walker.
I always knew I was her target.

Let's not begin this way,
instead, let's celebrate
as Whitman once did
the path of every mother and child

through the first gray light of dawn
to the water's edge
where you snap – a wave –
against my shore
and all is calm.

"And every atom belonging to me
as well belongs to you."

Grass

They'll know me
in the neighborhood
as the person
always big with baby,
growing skin like spring flowers
biking with a bulging belly
running till my infant tumbles out of me,
the fountains of milk
watering such fertile lawns –
yours, mother,
yours is the lawn that had no soil, brown grass,
but my grass is green
like your envy.

Family Of Infants

to Ira

You helped me make him,
but more than that
you helped me make myself
like his four year old blocks
I have grown, square by rectangle
up to the sky;
I can fly
out of my body
if I choose;
yet I'd rather be here, in bed, with you
making us
bake another baby.

And at night
when star-light illuminates
the worry wrinkles grown deeper in your forehead,
you are my baby
we're a family of infants
made
to love each other.

Remembering Fireflies

Today you would have been three,
but I had decided three years, nine months ago
never to know you
though you are known in my heart
as child number two.

It was a conscious decision
getting rid of you,
though I wonder, when your five year old
brother speaks of God,
or your two month sister's smile
electrifies the room,
why it was you, chosen
for the life of obsolescence;

and why anyone
should be chosen
to be cast off;
why the four year old
with leukemia
can't see her next birthday,
or the A.I.D.S. infant
will never creep or crawl.

And you –
whose heart fluttered like a firefly
were given the gift of eyes,
yet blinded
from life.

A Found Poem: The Ninth Month

to Louis

"What do you think
of your wife's pregnant body?"

"It's magic
the way the back arches
like a half-moon;
up front –
a perfect roundness
hard and sturdy;
the belly-button
juts out like a tiny rose.

And if you look hard enough. . .
the outline of an arm
rubbing against the flesh
like it is rowing
ready to paddle itself out of its sea
any moment."

Mothers and Grandmothers

Rape

A face
the size of a hand
shining out of the amniotic sea,
emerges, shrieks of indignation –
the air is too cold,
the light, wildly opaque,
the flesh so naked
easy to be raped by any hand
even its mothers'.

Burns

I dream of placing you
back in my body –
wish fulfillment.
You are me, the infant
bound in a mother's
warm cushion of a body;
and this mother loves you
she would do anything for you
even have the sunshine
saturate her skin
so that she be the one who burns
instead of burning.

Without Mother

How many bodies leave
before they have found
what they wanted,
despite the decades
of discovering and discarding
the eighty year old man
no better off
than the infant
who can't find his way
without mother.

Cancer

Day by day
the daughter watched her mother
give her body
up to the air,
the flesh, a flag
hanging from the mast of bones;

the daughter was a mother for a month
until the older woman
was mumbling gibberish
eating mush

ready to go back
into the wound.

A Fairy-Tale of Three Mothers

One was mean and ugly,
they wouldn't even call her
a witch;
hag was better
but even that wasn't enough
since her outside was simply moderately ugly,
but her insides
were brutal.
Not only did she scream,
she howled like a werewolf
and I was scared of being swallowed
or bitten
though in truth
she only bit
sometimes pulled my hair
and screamed profanities
out to the wind.
I got rid of her
as soon as I possibly could.

I found a pretty mother
pretty but dumb.
I didn't know she was so dumb
until she forgot to make me dinner
or bring me to school,
but she didn't scream
and bought me beautiful clothes
from Bloomingdale's.

I discarded the clothes
kept the mother
realizing
she was sometimes purposeful,
but mostly
I viewed myself as orphaned

until I had children
and found another mother
besides myself
for them.

She was fat and gruesome,
but kind and wholesome
and never cursed
only said, 'stupid'
sometimes.

But when I peeked behind her words
I realized how much of the world
was stupid in her eyes,
and dark and ugly;
it was too long before I realized
this mother could cook a wicked brew
which I wasn't about to eat.

So now I'm through with mothers.
I'm throwing them out
into the brambles and branches
of some terribly dark woods,
while I, on the other hand
have discovered the exit from this forest
and am lusting and mothering
in the light

After a Back Surgery

to my mother, Fran

You sit
like a heavy trunk on the bed;
your hands, fallen leaves
hang off the side,
the little blonde hair left on your head
is lonely for other branches.

You ask me to turn you over on your side,
too difficult.

It's easier to change seasons, even
rather than find the strength
to move you.

My roots were broken long ago,
now you ask me to come back
and feel how tender the earth is;

to feel the hole in your back
the tributaries of bones

so that I, in turn, may become a tree
for you to root in.

A Mother's Daughter

When Donna comes over for Shabbos lunch
the house defends itself against her
in thick, plastic-covered chairs.
She rips the plastic with her nails
spills orange stuffed cabbage
on her clean, white shirt;
makes me think of snapshots of her mother
sealed in like stances.
Words race out of her,
"Did mommy and daddy tell you I'm in the drama club?
oh, and I have a new boyfriend."
My husband is having such a good time
like he did when Lillian was fourteen.
Hair falls out of my net
I take a bath in my sweat,
stroke her golden hair
rub down the length of her backside
and kiss her mother's cheek.

Sounds

to my grandmother

All day
the leaves work hard
falling off the tree.

The night has clearly defined muscles,
emerges – panting and dark
falls – silent, blind;

and all that you can hear
are crickets
a careless linnet cries

my sleep
which floats up to the surface

recalling years ago
with grandma in the country

the sound of her heavy breathing
staining the air.

Kisses

I am your granddaughter through marriage.
In youth, I was always Frances' daughter.
(Lucky that she married a man with a child
or she would have been childless).

On birthdays I'd watch you nestle kisses
into the curls
on the heads of your grandchildren –
Jack's children, from birth.
I'd get cards signed, 'grandma K.'

Today, you are much smaller
than I ever was.
Your dying body
a mere ninety pounds.

Your gums
are old, dried up leaves.
Teeth swim aimlessly in a jar
on the side of the bed.

I know that I should kiss you,
but I can't.

On Giving my Grandmother a Shower

These are weeds –
fine, pubic hair
grown old;
a scar covers your swollen stomach
from which my mother emerged,
and I must scrub all of this
because you can no longer shower yourself,
bathe your swollen feet
where blue blood is ready
to break through the skin;
I soap up your back
afraid of the bones chipping apart,
afraid if I rub too hard that the flesh will fall off,
afraid I'll never get you
clean enough.

Songs

My dead grandmother
sits on a high perch
where no one can see her;

watches my stomach swell
hoping it will be a girl;
remembers the village women's songs
for death and also birth,

she had learned these songs from the wind
and they were really not different.

At the Park

The children are like deep-sea divers.
Every rock
is a remarkable discovery.
They fish in the sand-box
for treasures
pushing and shoving so hard
their parents leave;

great-grandmother Sadie
watches, slouched in her wheelchair,
her legs, dead driftwood.
She tries to imitate laughter
that once was hers.

Grandmother

She arrives
from where
the dead have slept.
Stands
in my living room
fatter than I remember her
dressed like the elders
in Russia
wide, black dress
babushka on her head;
her voice
pulses in my veins
especially when she says:
"I came to visit Kalman
the baby boy
you named after my dead son,
your father."

Nothing is worse
than when a son dies before his mother.

Children

To Woman With a Child

We've never said a word
yet we speak
through the infants
tied to our chests in slings;
they float in darkness
as we skim
the edges of sleep
listening to cries
that may be nameless.

On Babysitting For a Friend's Son

to Adam

I'm trying to find words for this poem –
empty. I write
while you sleep
in the other room
muttering secret sounds
to yourself.

Do such syllables
make any more sense
than my own?

I work hours
often taking no pleasure
in what I have said.

You sing softly to yourself
moving across the landscape of your crib
delighted
by the pillow
beneath your tiny head.

The Diaphragm

to Elizabeth

She dreamed
five year old thoughts
of what it was
her mother wouldn't tell her
till she was seventeen;

she imagined
its tiny plastic rim
round and perfect like a bulb;

what magic
locked inside.

And if she listened
hard enough
to the night
snapping in small ways
all around her,
could she discover
the light inside the white.

"What?" she asked.
Her mother answered,
"Wait. Wait until you're older."

"I know," she rejoiced
as she listened
to the stars let out a sigh;

"It's to make you smell pretty."

And
feeling perfectly satisfied with her answer
she slipped
into slumber.

Foreplay

to Craig and Josha

A sleepover
and you're itching
to get rid of the skin;
instead you grab his
you'd like to take a bite
and swallow his blood, his sweat,
his voice in your mouth;
but for now
a little rough wrestling
some hand and finger play
is enough.

Morning comes
dense with sunshine
two six year old boys
at play.

Midas' Touch

A new Midas, everything you touch:
Mr. Panda, Ms. Bird, the bottle
or my breasts tremble
beneath your tiny touch;
even my milk
is golden.

K.K.K.

I never had a son
who had to worry about the color of his face
in public,
but if, because of it,
some ghosts appeared
and hunted him
out of his body
he, who was my baby,
I'd only hope
they'd bake the ghosts in the ovens,
consecrated to the flames that eat them
lit by Mobil or Exxon;
it wouldn't matter
as long as it was slow.

A Parent's Nightmare

Illness.
Not the kind
you cure with a pill or simple
injection.
The one
which festers in the mind
where unfettered filaments float
without direction.
Nothing you can do or say
no gestures
to retrieve the past
can realign
his gravity.
Nothing.

Untitled

Mother puts on shirt
kisses the left shoulder
where there is no arm
only flesh
no longer than a finger.

Out to play,
he is followed by his
five year old shadow;
right arm swings full circle,
left arm
watches intently
little league players
hit fly balls.

He catches
the sunlight
through his open sleeve.

Meningitis

To wake up
childless,
when just the day before
you helped her string beads
sang her Mother Goose rhymes
where disaster
was the implied syllable,
'Jack fell down and broke his crown.'

In this life
everything breaks.
She is gone, taking nothing
without saying
good-bye.

A Woman and Her Lovers

He couldn't sleep
because of the noises
in the night:
heavy trucks, shrill breaks.
He kept tossing and turning
one side of him asleep,
the other side awake,
the wisp of blonde curls tickling his eyes,
and in his tiny ears
the heaving and shoving of his mother's sex
in the other room.

Turn Off the Light

Etan Patz
went to school
never came home.
He was five and blonde.

As my infant sleeps
his arms thrown overhead
like the sky
in his carriage;

I think about Etan
once resting
beneath the watchful eyes
of his mother
whose lips
wore a permanent smile,

and what it must be like
as she bids goodnight
to his empty bed
turns off the light.

Bruises

An infant fell
ten stories
pushed by a baby brother
or harassed parent
with ten kids
in a one bedroom apartment.

Nobody knew
the exact cause
though neighbors reported
the sidewalk was bruised
with blood.

Gifts

> to Joel Steinberg

You
are me
on the darkest, sleepless night
when stars are a mirage
and the burden of the next twelve hours
binds me in a straight jacket. I try
counting one star, then two and three
enraged
by how little there is out there;
and my son, he asks for me
two, three, twenty times
through all hours of darkness;
first it's milk, then it's bathroom,
soon it's every nightmare
from fear of cookies as large as moons
to torture by shadows. Enough.
Stop these hours
let day come,
but my son continues to cry
and out of my body steps this person
with hands as strong as lead.
I wrench my nailed fingers
around his little, helpless neck
till there's blood
on his teddy-bear;
like you did
to your six year old daughter
who, bruised and battered
was just declared brain-dead.

I could have been you
but as my son sleeps restlessly
like I, his mother,
I manage survival
with the gifts I've been given.

Disneyworld

to Ira and Craig

When you are in the air
two children –
father and son
dream filled and expectant
like the sun
ready to burst
through a heavy-cloud cover;
I only went to watch;

it's like star-gazing
on a black and brilliant night
knowing I could never shine as brightly
but could still be lifted.

About the World

You talk,
enamored of your sounds –
gibberish, with an occasional word
that's comprehensible.

I catch you in these soft
and quite unnoticed moments,
holding your stuffed dog
up in the air,
telling him all there is to know
about the world.

Cross Country Skiing, Pound Ridge, February 1988

to Craig

In these woods
it's hard to know
where clouds end
and land begins,
hard to know
where I end
my long, hard tracks
and you begin
your tiny, gentle ones,
and whose voice
is moving the branches –
the wind
or your three year old sounds.
Where are the edges?
Drifting, drifting
your footsteps in my footsteps
in the lullaby
of snow.

Distant Star

to Craig

You're climbing back
into my skin
which is filled
with an eight month old embryo.
It doesn't matter, you say
tugging at my flesh
like it's a weed
seeking out space
behind the shadows
in river beds,
already
feeling displaced
as the memory
of a distant star
in darkness.

Fallen Tooth

to Craig, Age Four

Fallen
into darkness,
your smile
no longer whole
but an absence
an aching
for completion;
while months from now
a new one
will emerge,
you'll still yearn
to be filled up
to be whole.

Simply Just

to Craig

For the first time
you saw your parents kiss
and smiled,
and said it was beautiful
because the woman who kissed your father
was his wife, not yours
nor could she ever be
anything but the woman
whose flabby, aged stomach
you plunged out of
seven years ago;
simply just
your mother.

Blind Batter

Sometimes I slip
over the edge
circling depths
only fish know
or vibrating between screams –
my own, turned loose;
often
you tumble into this space
and vibrate like a tornado
little thing that you are
how could you possibly understand
the fast pitches of the night
and its open mouth;
so you stand still as a blind batter at plate
frightened to move
near your mother.

Overboard

He can't keep
his joy
under-tow;
twenty years
from today
he'll have a woman trembling
overboard.

Pollen

to Samantha Rose, 22 months

We sit so close
I smell your heart-beat
and remember
that I gave it to you.
It doesn't matter
now that you're walking on your own;
I can smell you
like the perfect rose
whose middle name is yours,
but the blush of crimson
which shades your cheeks
is yours to throw
like pollen to the wind.

A Bike Ride with my Two Year Old

to Samantha Rose

Your little head
pressed against my back
like a tattoo
reminds me
of the brother before you
who'd sit on the back of my bike and sing
beneath the yellow, moving light
while settling
inside my skin
sleeping, waking, turning
the air.

My Daughter's Music

You hear it
and you're off,
swirling in the air
with fluid quickness
like a dolphin
squealing with delight
at the rhythms
of water
I don't hear
nor can I keep up with;

so I watch
listen
to the wild dancing in and out of waves.

The Naked Emperor

This
is your favorite holiday –
pretending to be
someone you're not,
not knowing who you are
you try on different masks.

Daughter,
any Sleeping Beauty can tell you
the spinning wheel hurts,
the blood is real
and sometimes H.I.V. positive;

everyone knows
the emperor
is naked.

After Halloween

to Craig, Age Nine

No more candy.
No more treats.
Unmasked,
exhausted
you fall into sleep
deeper and darker
than ever before.

The nightmares begin:
some of the monsters are real
the masks, permanent.
Yesterday in Brooklyn
some boys threw eggs;
an angry man stabbed the child.
He was nine.

This is no party;
the ghosts and goblins have arrived
for good.

It was blood on the ground
not make-up.

After Halloween II

to Samantha, Age Five

Costume off
you fall
into sleep
like a storm.

What a treat
to be such a loved mother
to be such a loved daughter.

Like Dreams

to Samantha, Age Five

Halloween
is a constant discussion in our house –
jack o' lanterns, treats,
tricks so mean
they lift the bones in the wind;

and costumes
which one to wear next year,
the year after that
as if
without this day
there is no magic in the air
or strange light
appearing and disappearing
in the early dark
of autumn
like dreams.

On the Evening of Halloween

to Samantha

When the clothes come off,
when darkness descends
darker than ever
and the ghosts and goblins come out;
when sleep comes to you
a gift God has given
and the costume lies like a heap on the floor –
that's when you are beautiful,
sleeping, naked
all five years of you
filled with dreams
that Halloween be every day;

while my treat
is watching you
asleep.

Home

to Samantha

Enjoy your body
like your house;
inhabit each room comfortably
sleep in your skin
with not an itch or a tremor;
enjoy your walls
while you walk through every room
with a feeling –
this is okay
to move here, to stay for coffee,
to stay forever
and invite someone, eventually
to share it with you.

Be Thankful for . . . .

to Ira, Craig, Samantha

The procession of breaths
your children inhale,
the plump happiness of their cheeks
of their smiles.
And your husband
you need no language to understand
his face, his body;
yet every morning
you are greeted by the history you share
a hello
the perfect human gesture.

You enjoy
the taste of freshly brewed coffee,
the NEW YORK TIMES,
words
on the other end of the wire
perhaps from another part of the universe
or maybe around the corner.
And behind each corner
is some magical, mysterious moment
awaiting your arrival
with hopeful wing-tips.
Dreams of your father waving, waving
sliding out of sight.
Be thankful for
morning
the first ray of light
you've made it through
another night.

About the Author

Pamela Laskin is a teacher, cyclist, walker, swimmer and avid reader. Many of her poems, short stories and children's stories have been published in journals and magazines. *Central Station*, her first book of poetry, was the winner of the Millennium Poetry Prize, and three other poetry chapbooks have been published as well as five picture books and two young adult novels. She recently edited, *The Heroic Young Woman*, a collection of original fairytales. She lives in Brooklyn, New York, with her husband, Ira. Her children, Craig and Samantha, are completing their degrees.

Acknowledgements

Acknowledgement is made to the following publications in which these poems first appeared

"Cross Country Skiing". . . *Bristlecone*
"At the Park". . . *Forum*
"Simply Just". . . *Joy of Journey*
"K.K.K". . . *Kindred Spirit*
"About the World" . . . *Languag/Processing*
"Blind Batter" . . . *New Song*
"The Abortion" . . . *New York Quarterly*
"Home"; "On the Evening"; "In the Womb"...*Poetry in Performance*
"Sounds" . . . *Promethean*
"Grandmother/Shower" . . . *Rebirth of Artemis*
"Daughter's Music"; "Pollen" . . . *Robin's Nest*
"Songs" . . . *Telewoman*
"Grandmother: . . . *www.thebluejewyorker.com*
"Fallen Tooth" . . . *Treasured Poems/America*

www.ingramcontent.com/pod-product-compliance
Lightning Source LLC
Chambersburg PA
CBHW071031080526
44587CB00015B/2567